EXPRESSIONS

A BOOK OF POETRY

MARIO GIVENS

EXPRESSIONS

@Copyright 2020 by MARIO GIVENS
All rights reserved. No part of this book maybe reproduced or transmitted in any form or by any means without written permission from the author.

ISBN: 978-1-953638-40-3

Printed in the United States of America

This book or parts thereof may not be reproduced in any form, stored in a retrieval system, or transmitted in any form by any means-electronic, mechanical, photocopy, recording, or otherwise-without prior written permission of the publisher, except as provided by United States of America copyright law.

**PUBLISHER
TA MEDIA & PRODUCTIONS LLC
DALLAS, TX 75240
www.PUBLISHYOURBOOKTODAY.INFO
WWW.TAMEDIACO.COM**

ACKNOWLEDGMENTS

I want to start off by saying we serve an awesome God. When there were days where I felt the need to give up, I came to him with my frustrations and he led me back on the road of greatness. To my children Nia and Mario Jr., you both give me the inspiration and motivation I need to make sure my dream stays true not only for me but for you both to have a legacy. To Tiffany A. Green-Hood and TA MEDIA + Co., thank you so much for always making my vision be shown through the eyes of the readers. We started this journey many moons ago and we are still here living our purpose.

A very special thanks to my mom Rhonda Givens for being so inspiring and patient throughout her trials with her health, I love you for being so strong and seeing that smiles brightens my soul. To my family and friends thank you all for the support you have given me during this process. Thank you to all the people who supported me on all social media outlets because my goal is to reach many people in the world. May God bless everybody journeys, seasons and purpose.

DEDICATION

I want to give a very special thanks to my mom Rhonda Givens for being so inspiring and patient throughout her trials with dealing with her health. I love you for being a strong black woman. When I see your smile it brightens up my soul. Thank you for always believing in me and my abilities when I don't have enough in me to finish. I love you for being a strong black woman. May God continue to bless your warm heart and soul.

INTRODUCTION

If you are in need of a moment to relax your mind, then this book will give you that feeling. When reading this poetry, you will take your mind on a peaceful voyage through the stories that is being told. This book will contain real life stories through poetry and many readers can relate based critical life experiences. In all honesty this book will give that moment to not only reflect what you are going through but what the author has been through.

TABLE OF CONTENTS

SLEEPING UNIVERSE 1
SOUL TIE 2
LONELY CRATER 3
ETERNAL LOVE 4
BULLET 5
HAVE YOU EVER CRIED? 6
I HAD TO BELIEVE 8
A BRIEF THOUGHT 10
DREAMING OF REALITY 11
FLOWER 13
GUIDANCE 14
TOURING FOREVER 15
DRAGON LOVE 16
SOULLESS MATE 17
A THOUGHTFUL SIP OF WINE 18
HEARTBREAKING RAIN 20
SPECIAL GIFT 21
BROKEN ANGEL 22
HE WAS SO HURT THAT NIGHT 23
READING MYSELF 24
DESTINY OF LOVE 26
LONGING FOR LOVE 27
ASLEEP 28

IF ONLY I COULD TAKE A TRIP TO THE SUN	29
I WILL ALWAYS LOVE YOU	31
BLUE SKY	32
QUESTIONABLE PERFECTION	33
I'M ME	34
INTENTIONAL	36
BRITTLE	37
CARVED	38
POSTCARD	39
PEACEFUL THINKING	40
SLOW DANCE	41
I'M FREE	42
SHE'S SO DELICATE	43
GODS BEAUTIFUL SCULPTURE	44
BROKEN SUN	45
I KNOW YOU ARE HERE	47
DYING DOVES	48
ALWAYS HERE	49
BEDTIME	50
A LOVE FREQUENCY	51
BROKEN PIECES	52
MOON AND SUN CHRONICLES	53
BUTTERFLY AGAIN	55
IMPERFECT LOVE	56
WRITER'S SUICIDE	57

A KISSABLE MOMENT	59
A DYING THOUGHT	60
MOSCATO	61
CRYING BOY	63
DEEP THOUGHT	65
THE END	67
UNBALANCED SOULS	68
SPEED OF HAPPINESS	70
EVERLASTING THOUGHTS	71
BROKEN SWIM	72
SHATTERED	73
INVISIBLE PURPOSE	74
A DEADLY WORLD	75
FOCUS	76
MADE LOVE	77
HURT AND HAPPINESS	79
QUEST TO FIND YOUR HEART	80
COLD ARROW	81
MISSING LOVE	82
HOPELESS ROMANCE	83
A SAD DREAM	84
CORAL SPIRIT	85
POOR NEGRO	86
DEATH TO LOVE	88
A SHACKLED HEART	89

A PEACEFUL DREAM	90
INNER OCEAN	91
BEGINNING OF THE END	92
MENTAL STORM	93
JOYFUL	94
A CRYING DEED	95
DIFFERENT SEASONS	97
BARE FLOOR	98
DEAR EARTH	100
YOU ARE	102
A DREAM OF CLOSURE	103
MENTALLY TOGETHER	105
GEMINI CHRONICLES	106
FALL SEASON	108
LETTER TO CUPID	109
A LOVABLE PURPOSE	110
SAVORING LOVE	111
(FT. POET ALIADA DUNCAN)	111
FALLING PROMISE	114
WINSTON SALEM	116
MR POET	117
SAND	119
LIVING DREAM	120
RELAXING BATH	121
WOMAN	122

THAT FEELING 123
LOST BATTLE 124
PROTECTION 126
DEAR LOVE 127
FAR TOUCH 129
CRY TO SLEEP 130
THOUGHTFUL EYES 131
APOLOGETIC HEART 132
FOREVER DREAM 133
FINAL KISS 135
CRASHING UNIVERSE 137
DYING VOICE 139
UNEXPECTED FEELINGS 142
SLEEPLESS SEX 144
GODS HANDS 146
GUITAR STRINGS OF LIFE 148
A HUMBLE DEATH 149
CHAOTIC DREAMS 151

SLEEPING UNIVERSE

I'm waiting for you to arrive
This planet is empty without you
I've thought about you for so long
I seen the sun turn into the moon
These days are scaring me
It seems like I'll be alone in this empty world
Did destiny travel to another galaxy?
Now the stars have changed their shapes
The universe lied to me
I can't get you out of my mind
I visioned making love to you as we created storms
Planet earth will understand my passion for you
My kisses will have you flood the soil
The season of spring produces flowers
Your moans communicate through the air
The wind understands stability
I'm patient to wake up from a dream
Knowing I loved you in my mind at the time when my soul is at rest.

SOUL TIE

I made love to your soul

Then I left a part of my chemistry inside your physics

The connection was intimate

I can't seem to let you go

I'm addicted to your life

Your presence completes my heart

Our journey together will last forever

Knowing both of our souls made love.

LONELY CRATER

I took a long trip to the moon

Then I found a crater to lounge in

All I was doing was thinking

Placing my feelings onto another crater

Then my heart stop

I was wondering why I'm so hurt

Then sadness consumes my soul

I begin to cry

As each tear fell

Rain travels from the sky

Now the earth can feel my pain

Creating weeds in the gardens of beautiful flowers

My spirit hurts so bad

I rather be lost in a galaxy of calm

Where all I have is the stars to brighten up my darkness.

ETERNAL LOVE

If I died tonight and when I got to heaven

The next day I'll send a butterfly to fly to you

That way you know I will always love you.

BULLET

As I left home
I didn't realize my house was on fire
I was confused by my purpose
My mind flies into a place of uncertainty
I don't have control of my own destiny
Where will I go?
I'm homeless
I'm lost trying to find a home
Then I look up
I saw a young black man flinching
I decided to pay rent in his chest
Then I heard a loud hurtful scream
Not knowing the sound came from the back room of his lungs
He fell to the ground slowly
All I can feel is the wetness from the blood rain
What just happen?
What did I do?
I just wanted a place to rest
I never wanted to harm anyone.

HAVE YOU EVER CRIED?

Have you ever cried?
Shed tears from the what's, how's and why's
Confuse from the heartbreaks of others
I never been this hurt
So hurt that my tears never fell
They stayed inside my eyes
They are Afraid to run because they knew they will die
Everything I feel saddens my heart
I'm in cardiac arrest
Death came because the lack of CPR
Then I grasp for air
Wait I'm alive
It was my thoughts that form the conclusion of death
So now my eyes are open
I can see the love
I can taste the hate
The feelings are too much to bear
I have to leave
My heart and soul are fighting for supremacy

The battle to regain strength is tough
There is too much pain to endure
Then I stop at this very moment
I began to take a deep breath
I began to realize one particular thing
Friendships is a voluntary value
It holds a place in my spine
Then I visualize that pain is something I have control.

I HAD TO BELIEVE

I've definitely been hurt
It's not your typical heart break
I lost my worth
I was Shattered
Mentally demolished
I didn't feel the man inside of me
No words could console me
My thoughts were depressed by pain
It left an emotional stain
I wanted to bleach my heart
Inject my soul with a new start
I cried so much that my tears didn't run
I'm so tired
Exhausted from lost energy
I just wanted happiness
There was no motivation for me
The only inspiration I had was the possibilities
Then I realize there was no opportunities
What I'm going to do?
I felt I was toxic

It's hard when you face the truth
So I prayed
Prioritize my days
Set many goals
Removed all my negative ways
Then a voice appeared
It whispers prophecies in my ears
I listened
I was told to stop being distant
Take chances on life
Maximize your flight
Your journey just begun
Then my smile came
My confidence wasn't ashamed
The evolution of my life is so beautiful
I will take heed
I was on a path of greatness
I just had to believe.

A BRIEF THOUGHT

Can I express a sentence?
Deposit my heart into your spirit
Would you withdrawal my love?
Then purchase a lifetime of togetherness.

DREAMING OF REALITY

Once upon a night
I fell in love with my dreams
Then she appeared
It's like she came in my clouds
I can see my thoughts while my eyes are closed, and it seems
very clear
She can be my soulmate
Only when I'm sleep I can vision her
I'm counting hearts instead of sheep
Every night my thoughts gets deeper
Then my vision plays many movies
We begin to go on many dates
Some nights we make love in many places
Her smile grasps my soul
She's so secure when I'm near her
Then I get real sad
It's only when my eyes are open
I don't see her no more
I just sit and start daydreaming about her
Now I'm trying to work hard so I can get tired

That way I can fall asleep so I can dream of her
Take her on a vacation
Sip on some red wine
Hugging and kissing her
We are so relaxed
I start to look into her eyes
This woman is so beautiful
The earth is so balance when she smiles
My heart beats with a rhythm of love
It plays a seductive song
I now have the courage to be her man
Then I woke up again
These dreams are telling me a story
The thoughts of her motivates me
It's like a cup of warm lavender tea
My days are so relaxing
Only if the world knew how much she gives me peace
Then reality sets into my spirit
These dreams may come to an end
Then I'll be having nightmares of her
Wondering how life would've been.

FLOWER

As I sit and wonder

How could life be this calm

Then I realize you were here

Just sitting

Smelling the roses that was planted by your feet

A queen sits on her throne of love

The hummingbird's whispers peace to your ears

The bees kiss you knowing you are sweet like honey

I'm calm and relax

Your spirit is like an orchid

That I planted in my garden of trust.

GUIDANCE

It was a dreadful night out

The moon was silent

A cold brisk of wind blew into my lungs

I couldn't wait to go home and pray

My mind is clog with many thoughts

I have to be careful of the words I say

So I corrected my intentions

Place my heart into God's hands

I'm giving him full control

I need my soul to comprehend

The confusion needs to go away

Then patience took over me

It's enough room for clarity

I refuse to be lost in a space of uncertainty

My thoughts have thoughts

I need to release this pain my lord

Before I get up my head kiss the floor

At that moment I knew God would guide me to peace.

TOURING FOREVER

Please know my feelings are sincere

It's like traveling to a secluded place

A sacred space

To only realize that one of us are alone

A single trip without a special person

One heart subtracts another

I'm far from happiness

Peace is my ultimate destination

Can you meet me at the gate?

I want to go on a forever tour with you.

DRAGON LOVE

I felt the moment where betrayal conquer my mind

It was a devastating time in my life

You left me without warning

I can't focus on my accomplishments

It felt like fire was blowing from your mouth

A sense of being burned by deceit

Then I saw the anger when you roar your explanation

Love was hurt by the disrespect

I never thought I would feel this way

Then the fire came again

What did I do that bad?

You supposed to be my protector

Your wings supposed to keep the danger away

Now you are the danger

It's like I fell inside a deep pool, a dark cave

I just pray you will fly far away

To give me the opportunity to heal

Then I realize no matter what happens

Your fire branded my soul.

SOULLESS MATE

My tears stop falling
I'm in a state of broken hearted
The love is where it all started
She's gone now
A friend decided to end a forever bond
It was an insensitive moment
She seemed so subhuman
Callous became her alter ego
I never would've thought she could be unsympathetic
The pain and hurt she left me
It's like she became heartless
What made her decline my love?
Can her soul regain the passion she had for me?
I'll wait a lifetime to have that attachment again
Hopefully one day her soul won't be less without me.

A THOUGHTFUL SIP OF WINE

The rhythm in my heart trembled erratically as I saw your smile light up a room full of love

I glanced outside the windows to notice that the sun was going to sleep

It was like you were reminding the sun that there's only one light and you will shine brightly

I sit here and I wonder what's on your mind as you sip your wine

Hopefully, it's a thought of you whispering something short and pleasant in my ear

Maybe a warm hug to showcase a sense of security

I value a woman with a voice that brings so much calm to the storms

You are a beautiful soul that has a radiant smile and eyes that are very mesmerizing

If only you knew what was going on in my thoughts as I sip on my wine

Thinking about how special you are

It's like you are an angel flying free without any worries

I will respect your landing when I know It would be on my platform of love.

HEARTBREAKING RAIN

It was a warm summer day

Then I expected rain was near

The clouds begin to form and the sky was dark

I need to seek some shelter

The thunder pounds the earth

Shaking the foundation

As lightning illuminates the sky

It begins to pour heavily

The ground is flooded

I got caught in a rainstorm

She left me alone

I didn't know she was leaving me when she found another home.

SPECIAL GIFT

Many moons ago I visualize a woman like you
Your beauty is a ray from the moon to the lake
The shine is your smile
The water is calm
I do admire you
Wishing I could shoot my arrow into your heart
Then your eyes told me many stories
You have skin of ancient queens
I'm mesmerized by your grace
I want you in my space
Holding hands while we glance
Communicating feelings of love
You are very special
A present that I hope God created for me
Now my day is made when I see you
Maybe one day I can be with you
Show you a king with many qualities
A man with possibilities
I can be a Gift from God to you.

BROKEN ANGEL

I broke your wings

My intentions were not to harm your flight

I disrespected the air you needed to fly

You didn't deserve this

Can you forgive me?

I going to miss your sincerity

You completed my purpose

I took your calling for granted

The tears you shed flooded my thoughts

Every feather was your loyalty to me

Each soar meant you had trust in me

Then I failed you

I didn't execute what a man supposed to do

I know when it's your time to land

Hopefully you would've forgave me

When your claws grab the earth.

HE WAS SO HURT THAT NIGHT

He was so hurt that night
His ability to live was at a standstill
Many thoughts cross his mind
His soul created an emotion of fright
How could someone break a heart of love
It was determined he would forget his goals
The look upon his face as he walks my way
I wanted to ask him was he okay
Then I notice the tears running down his face
He was in an awkward place
Confusion became his personality
I hope he snaps out that mental state
He needs to change his spiritual space.

READING MYSELF

I came from a mindset that consists of poverty
Numerous broken thoughts
Pain that consumes my mind
I let too many people in
They were so close
I still wouldn't let them comprehend
I'm protecting my words
My sentences need closure
I lost many paragraphs
Distant myself from verbs
Many commas didn't follow words
I had to reread the table of contents
Put everything back into its proper place
I place my safe inside a safe
I'm obsess with guarding my world
I have to protect my feelings
Then secure my emotions
I don't need vulnerability anymore
Contentment reach a level of chances
I'm just free

Gratification fell in love with satisfaction
Dreams disregarded reality
I'm so bless
Determine to reach a place that only is right for me
This secluded island has palm trees that reminds me of love ones
The water is clear like the people that surrounds me
Taking these moments to sit in a beach chair
Clearing mental space as each wave kiss the shoreline
I'm home
I took time out to read a book
When I got to the end
The glossary defines all my faults and great moments
I place myself on a shelf of greatness.

DESTINY OF LOVE

Destiny prevailed that night when I held your hand

I felt a sense of closure from your energy

It was a complicated moment to comprehend

I found my reason to love again

You made my heart have that piece of peace

I can rest knowing I have that security

My future has a purpose

All because my present had patience.

LONGING FOR LOVE

Having the inability to produce an emotion can hurt you more than the other person
Then I open my mind up to the ability to love again
I had to go back into my past to see what made me feel this way
At this point my heart wasn't accessible to be pure and warm
Then I brought my thoughts back to the present moment
It's time to unseal the feelings I have for myself
I've been anxious long enough to realize my deserving heart needs love
I'm very confident and eager to see my future with the woman that god created for me.

ASLEEP

I fell asleep last night

When I woke, I realize the dream was over

That it was a magical illusion

I disappear from the life of confusion

I'm back in the world of shelter

Securing my heart from past pain

The hurtful pain that lives inside of me

That same pain that haunts my present

I have to conquer that pain

My future needs a change

Then I went to sleep to wake up knowing my pain ends

All I needed was a cup of spiritual tea.

IF ONLY I COULD TAKE A TRIP TO THE SUN

If only I could take a trip to the sun
I know the rays would burn
Leaving a tan that will last internally into my spirit
At that moment I was warned
When I look at the sun
I was blinded by the fire
My soul was shunned
Then the day got confusing
Many clouds calmed the sky
It was very amusing
Then the sun lost power
So I decided to take a trip
As I got closer to the sky
The air was getting thinner
Making it hard to breathe
Now I was losing power
I need to rejuvenate my soul
Then the clouds remove themselves from the situation

The sun was getting frustrated

It produces more rays

I'm in the middle of the sky

Wondering what should I do

Then the clouds came again

I'm getting closer and closer

The voyage is getting less confusing

The clouds took a long time to move

Then the air begins to get thicker and cool

The sun disappeared

It changed into the moon.

I WILL ALWAYS LOVE YOU

I will always love you
There is not a day goes by
Even when the sun goes down
I will always love you

When the moon shines the night
I will always love you
The birds sing in the morning
I will always love you

As the lakes goes down stream
I will always love you
I'm just a little worried
When the storm is over
Will you always love me?

BLUE SKY

I am the sky where the clouds are the people who lives in my world. Every time the wind blows many clouds floats away leaving me waiting for the next people to encounter.

QUESTIONABLE PERFECTION

One's goal is to have the ultimate life
The birds chirping
The squirrels climbing trees
You know that sound of buzzing bees
When everything goes as plan
You can't have a bad day
It's like every word you speak is sincere
The kids in the park happy when they play
Life is full of warm cheer and glee
Your eyes are the protection of the energy you see
When you are in love the kisses are slow and warm
Every touch has a soft secure feeling
Just for the sake of thought
What if you could not have those things?
Would life be a bad thing?
Would you still function in the mist of uncertainty?
Can you function without the voices that sing?
We tend to want the best, then we overlook the present
Knowing the best was not perfection, but the effort of just being happy.

I'M ME

Do you really know me?
My thoughts were hidden for a reason
Then I allowed my heart to open
I let many come inside my soul
Hoping they will handle me with care
I was really scared
My anxiety created a moment of nervousness
I'm thinking many will hurt me
Leave me in a mental space of sadness
So I prayed
Put my heart into god's hands
Allowing him to guide my life
Then I allowed many more people into my world
I wasn't scared anymore
The lesson was taught
I understood my journey
Many will love you and many will hurt you
I have to balance my emotions
Then accept my season
Put my trust into patience

Many answers will define why I'm here
I've evolved into my purpose.

INTENTIONAL

If you love me like you say you do
Then why would you take my energy?
To use it to destroy my ability to love another
Your purpose was to hurt with the shadow of love.

BRITTLE

Can I trust you with my heart?
Without you dropping it into a puddle of deceit
It's fragile like a vase missing its flowers
The blood flows through my body because of trust
My soul cries out for help from the pain of being alone
It is moments where I can't function
Thinking and hoping for a calm spirit
So please be patient with my heart
I'm still trying to put this puzzle back together
If you are the missing piece to my life
Make sure you bring the peace to keep my heart together.

CARVED

I feel like a kid again

Standing next to this tree

My thoughts of carving a heart into it

The deeper I cut the heart

It symbolizes my love for you

So why I'm standing here crying?

I finally realize I have no name to write my love too.

POSTCARD

Our love we share have warmth

It's like taking a picture standing in front of mountains

Embracing one another with a kiss

Every pose captures our love for one another

We are a landmark for togetherness

A perfect picture that had a perfect moment

The frame is the foundation that gives us forever.

PEACEFUL THINKING

I'm so relax laying in this grass
A short vision as if you pass
My mind is distracted by your beauty
You just didn't cross my thoughts
You became the words to my speech
I fell in love with the opportunity
Then I glance at the scenery
I'm missing your scenery
You became my tranquility
The reason I have sanctuary
This is not the time to cry
I'm so happy by the fact you crossed my mind
I have an empty soul
Only you can fill my heart
When you accept my love.

SLOW DANCE

Can I have this dance?
Let's take a trip to the dance floor
The music is playing a slow tune
I can see the glow in your eyes
I'm going to lead her to the rhythm of the beat
I place my right hand on her lower back
My left hand holds her right hand as I guide her
We gave each other a quick smile
She's safe now inside my arms
It's like we are glued together in harmony
The cadence of the song creates a lovable movement
We are one with this tempo
Each step forward brings happiness and joy
Every step backwards shows a sense of bliss
As the song gets closer to the end
Our smiles showcase a delightful look
The song has ended then we release our embrace
Can this be an opportunity of future love?
After I shook off this daydream
I think I'm going to ask her do she want to dance.

I'M FREE

I'm free like the birds when they take flight

I'm free like the fish when they swim down stream

I'm free like a star shining next to the moon

I'm free like a cloud in a thunderstorm

Most importantly I'm free because my heart fell in love with life.

SHE'S SO DELICATE

Her skin is valuable like a queen on a throne
I'm committed to her feet
I want to kneel down to her for instructions
I only face sadness when she's gone
I face the moment of being alone
My mind is distant from the world
I'm lost with her motivation
It's like being stuck alone on an island without inspiration
Life is empty when she's not in my presence.

GODS BEAUTIFUL SCULPTURE

Her eyes are remarkable

They give the world the vision we need to see

The sun hides behind the clouds

A smile that brightens up days where the storms commands

Her skin is radiant like clay from inside the palm of god hands

She had a face that lives forever in a frame

She's picture perfect

Her beauty is so angelic

All she is missing are her wings.

BROKEN SUN

My rays have no strength
The power within me has died
The earth I secure remains dark
When I shine on top of the lake
The waves remain calmed
I'm so weak
You can see through the clouds
It's like the birds don't fly
I lost my purpose
I can't give the crops their will
This must be the end of my destiny
I don't know why I'm failing
I'm getting close to set
My life hasn't changed
The darkness is getting closer
I didn't service my purpose
My calling was to protect the earth in the day
So when the night comes it's peaceful
The calling was deceitful
When I begin to rise this morning

It seems like I'm weaker

I don't have faith anymore

I need the moon to kiss my pain away.

I KNOW YOU ARE HERE

As the bird's soar
I can feel your presence
As the bees buzzed
I can smell your scent

As the wind blows
I can hear your words
As the dog's barks
I can feel your touch

As the kids play
I can see your smile
As the squirrels climbed the trees
I can understand your thoughts

No matter what happens on the earth
I know you are here with me
You live inside of me
You are the matriarch of my heart.

DYING DOVES

Please be patient with my heart

It's so fragile

I can't afford a feeling like this

It's like anything can create a shattered moment

My tears have no reasoning of why it's happening

It hurts so bad, that it feels like doves are dying inside me

I have no flight to get well

I'm so empty with concerned

Love is a dangerous emotion

It can make you feel like the doves are dying inside

I don't feel love anymore

My spirits had descended into the clouds

I'm so hurt by this pain

I just want the doves to come alive again.

ALWAYS HERE

When you decide to cry

I'll be here

Whenever you are alone

I'll be here

When the smiles turn into frowns

I'll be here

When you have the feeling to give up

I'll be here

When you don't have the strength to fight anymore

I'll be here

Whenever you open your eyes

You will see it's you that's here.

BEDTIME

When I lay in my bed last night

My tears turned my pillow into an ocean

I'm drowning in my own hurt

It's the only thing that knows my pain

It feels my sorrow when I tussle every night

I have nightmares because my pillows wasn't fluff by you

My blankets give me a little calm

I have lost my peaceful dreams

It's times where I can't get no sleep

When will this pain ends?

The only relief is when I start my day

I'm afraid to lay down and get some sleep.

A LOVE FREQUENCY

The vibration of the earth doesn't have the same frequency without you walking by my side
It's like I can't hear the same sounds since you are not the ears next to me
My spirit fluctuates like waves in the ocean when you are not around
I will remain optimistic that one day my soul will have a calm rhythm
I'm confident you will come back into my life.

BROKEN PIECES

I'm broken into many pieces

My emotional puzzle is confused

Where do I start to heal?

I keep trying to put things together

The smile pieces don't fit the sad piece

My heart is so broke that it won't form a shape

All that is visioned are the shapes of pieces made out of a glass.

MOON AND SUN CHRONICLES

The moon cries and hides
The clouds cover her pain
The sun disrespected the day
She can't perform her daily duties
Her purpose took a pause
The sun didn't shine like god told him
He wasn't humble but still produce warmth
She wanted a perfect night
Now her workload is overloaded
Stress out from all the energy use to keep the universe complete
The sun wants forgiveness
He connected energy to the moon
He will do better
Light the sky and keep the clouds away
The moon must calm the earth
The sun needs to produce the earth
Will the moon forgive the sun?
Did the sun understand God's plan?

When they sun understands his role then it will make the moon job easier.

BUTTERFLY AGAIN

She appeared again

I never thought I would see her again

When I saw her, I can see a slight change

She wore different colors than before

A beautiful blue that looks like the sea when the sun shined

on it

I haven't been this excited

Her aura gave me this sense of tranquility

She has an elegant persona with her flight

A touch that's so soft, it's like you can't feel her

Her eyes are keen to where she wants to sit

She is so beautiful

The green on her back is like a tree full of leaves

I just hope she don't leave

I can't take another heartbreak

When she leaves, she leaves me in a dark place.

IMPERFECT LOVE

When I fell in love with you, it was because you had many flaws.
I would've walk away if you were perfect because that means we couldn't grow together through our hardships.

WRITER'S SUICIDE

I have so many thoughts in my head

But instead of saying never mind

I'll just express them

It's easier to release the energy that consumes me

Its where I have no strength

Then others tell me what to do

The same others that never knew

Telling me how to deal with fear

They don't have a clue

Google cannot cure me

Google not inside my head

But instead of never mind

I guess I just need to pray

Put my trust into a being

While carnal one's prey

What are my symptoms?

I was diagnosed with an issue to be judge

Then many say they love

To only turn around and disrespect the same thoughts that consumes me

So am I wrong to feel alone?

When I'm with people I'm alone anyway

I'm lost in my own head

But instead of never mind

I'll just find the remedy

I have my own prescription to anxiety.

A KISSABLE MOMENT

It was a magical kiss

The moment pauses

Everything around me froze

I was mesmerized by your trust

Each second I was at peace

I'm stuck inside your eyes

Nothing else even matters

I felt safe with your embrace

I'm grateful I have you

When I open my eyes

I'll cherish your kiss forever.

A DYING THOUGHT

Have you ever swim in your mind with someone?
You love them so much that they drowned you with their deceit
The only lifeguard is the protection of your heart
Then you grasp for air
Your body needs cpr
I'm in cardiac arrest
I need someone to resuscitate me
I can't breathe with all this negative energy in my lungs
Will someone rescue me?
I need them to push love into my heart
I'm grasping for more air
It's like I'm dying not knowing if love gave up on me.

MOSCATO

This is a different feeling

Words can't describe this moment

I'm speechless with thoughts

The similar thoughts that one can say is call intoxication

Mesmerized by the possibility

The visions I'm facing

I take a sip of her wine

The taste sparks touch

As my hands rubs her face

I lean closer

Kissing her in that special place

Her lips are soft

But I pause

What I'm doing

Should I continue to drink her wine

Her cup is full

Natural ingredients

Organic with every sip

Every glass taste good

We look in each other eyes

As I Whisper deep words into her ears
But why I keep tasting her WINE
More thoughts cross my mind
Words still can't explain this feeling
Visions of a queen
She's so fine
Her body is the perfection of an angel that flew across the sky
As She stands barefoot
With toes that's pretty like a vase of roses
More sips
I can smell the fragrance
An erotic feeling as the scent produce passion
Aroma of elegance
Move in on another chance
Making love inside her sutter home
An evening of romance
It's like Moon lightening
An effort of trying
The love turns into lust
Last call for another taste
A night to remember
A designated driver in her place.

CRYING BOY

Do you all really listen when I speak?
The voices come from a place so deep
Many wonders where my passion comes from
It's from the little boy who weeps
That same little boy who couldn't sleep
A child wasn't protected from the bruising
The mental ruining
I'm Stuck in a place where food was scarce
Where surviving came from educating my brain
That was the only time I had food for my thoughts
So now I'm full of being inspired
But my back had welts
Siblings couldn't understand what I felt
The pain became numb
The tears didn't run
They were stuck in a home behind my eyes
My strength evolves from being weak after no help
So, whatever happen to that boy?
Did he healed from the scars that was left internally?

The same boy who wanted to die so he didn't have to suffer

from the hurt inside

The Lies that was created when he cried

The truth wasn't free because his story was hidden like

slaves in barns

So where is that little boy who cried?

Did he ever heal?

I am the little boy who cried writing my pain so you all can

see my strength

The words I write is my medicine

I'm healed though nouns and verbs.

DEEP THOUGHT

I'm Deep in thought
Only I have the answers
The questions bring sentences
Parentheses follows
Many words won't describe
I can't end with a period
Pause from a comma
That brings exclamations to the gravity of my soul
The wonders of the creation of the earths soil
Genesis stills exists
As the wind blows challenges
Hurdles of life
Only a few can jump and reach the peak of greatness
As others trip into confusion
Leaving obstacles of trying
Lack of ambition
Not inspire to be motivated
Should I die into an ignorant coma?
Many can wake up into a conscious of truth
But the lies have a melody that stings from a flute

The wonders flow like the rivers that feeds the dry lands.

THE END

Destiny came and established its reasoning

My journey took its course

I've fulfilled my purpose for being here

I left smiles and many tears

It's time to move on to a better life

Take my wings and fly to another world

Then plant my claws onto the surface

It's time to establish new principles

I'm going to create a new purpose

I'll make sure I define my calling

When I look back at earth

I'll say my past didn't inflict pain into my future.

UNBALANCED SOULS

It was a cold and brisk night
The moon was hiding behind some clouds
You couldn't even see no stars
The sky was midnight black
The Darkness controlled the moment
The only sounds were the trees waving
Then I heard an owl speak its truth
The moment becomes a situation
Then the moon peaks as the clouds moves east
Now the night begins to live
The wind blows energy throughout the night
It has been an indescribable hour
Time is now ticking at a rapid pace
What can come from this confusing point in time?
It's a strange occurrence
I can hear howling at the moonshine
The spirits are possessed by the way the world being demented
Could this be a sign of uneasy tension?
We only have a few more hours left to daylight

As I watch from the window
I need to be more patient during this unbalanced time
Maybe the sun will shine some peace on their souls.

SPEED OF HAPPINESS

The world kept spinning slowly
It gave me an opportunity to think
I saw myself laying alone
Trying to find the proper words to speak
I can't understand where my life is going
It seems like everything went wrong
I sometimes feel like Cupid reverse back into the sky
Then put his bow back behind his wings
The failure came so rapidly I couldn't even try
When I finally snap out of it, I realize the world went faster
I can't seem to catch up
The speed of happiness continues to move at a rapid pace
What can I do to catch my purpose?
Will I ever get to the destiny of happiness?
Then something drastically happens
I fell to my knees with redemption
Then world begins to slow down
I realized that my blessings are manifested
When I prayed to god for his guidance
Then he grants me the opportunity to be happy forever

EVERLASTING THOUGHTS

It's days like this where I want to run and find a cave

That way I can scream and cry all day

So, when the night come, I'm so weak and I can get some sleep

I'm Exhausted from the strained of my brain

Just Overthinking what I can and will do if I get stress

My soul is a little press

So, this cave hides my emotions

Keeps my feelings in check

It's like I'm a zombie sitting overthinking

I'm so mentally tired

That my heart refuse to beat for the ones who I once loved

It's like my eyes can't see the harm no more

I'm dead to the pain that was inflicted in my spirit

This beautiful cave became my comfort zone

Only the bats show me love as they fly closer to my aura

I'm safe and I'm calm

Never distracted until reality sets in again

I have to live in this world until my cave is the pearly Gates.

BROKEN SWIM

The water is cold

It has waves that slowly moves me forward

Every stroke brings me a peace of mind

I feel free from the world

When my face goes underwater

I find myself gasping for air

Then I realize I can't swim

I'm drowning from my thoughts

I need a life raft to save my mind.

SHATTERED

My heart is like a vase falling off the bookshelf
I'm in multiple pieces of pain
This is a feeling I can't bare anymore
Many of my past memories cried so deeply
It's like I'm an umbrella lost in the trees
As I lay here all shattered without anyone helping
My words couldn't pronounce sentences
Too many Paragraphs of my mind were incomplete
My eyes had so many visions of what love should be like
My Glasses are crack from the damaging pictures
There's so much Confusion because of my internal fears
I can hear so many different voices so my ears disrespects voices
My Lips evicted speeches of my mind
I was hopeful to get a refund on the key to my heart
It's starting to feel like the storm will be over
As I look up for help, I notice my umbrella falls in my hands
I can be dry from the shelter that protects me from my own suffering

INVISIBLE PURPOSE

I left my shadow behind

I only walk alone

A slight distant mentality

I only understand myself

I'm Quiet from the chaotic world

My vision is blinded

I can't hear the voices of negativity

I'm invisible to one's sight

You can only feel my presence

When my soul leaves its legacy

Then you will be able to understand my reasoning

That my spirit will last forever in your hearts

My purpose was sincere to the world.

A DEADLY WORLD

Many tears were shed
No puddles were form
The moisture was dead
It was a dry storm
Only the wind blew cries
The hollering presented why's
Then darkness controls the night
The moon hid behind the clouds
The earth is hurt
Pain consumes the hearts
A soul leaves its home
His eyes are the windows with no blinds
The only remains are the stains he left on the ground
Then they flush his connection away
He descended to his purpose
A legacy short from longevity
The next day we will reread this poem
Knowing another soul leaves his soul on the ground.

FOCUS

I'm so lost

I find myself standing next to a tree

Then I become one with the bark

I can visualize my pain in my present

Then I froze for a second

I started to realize my past was a story

That my future will become glory

I perfected the NOW

I will never change the creation known as me

The race to the finish line showcases many triumphs

My journey was complete

When I stayed in my lane in the race of life.

MADE LOVE

The way your patience awaits when I insert my eagerness
I can feel your curiosity as I secure your emotions
The chemistry we share creates physics
Your hands write my ejaculations
Then each wet peck sends signals to my lower strength
I slowly caress your inner world forming storms and the thunder pounds
The moment is like swimming in the warmest river
My eyes close to dream about the reality
Our bodies are colliding to the earth blessings
The moon remains humble as my lips discuss erotic words to your hips
Your eyes are open to see my head tasting your spiritual honey
A slow rub on my head produces more nectar
Then your moans silence the night
As your nails carve your love into my back
Our skin become one then each slow stroke controls your body

The moans get intense to where my hands hold your arms behind your head
We both have a respectable orgasm as we lay weak in this bed
Love was made and now we can sleep knowing that our souls connected.

HURT AND HAPPINESS

Sometimes lust can have sex with love
Then impregnates confusion inside of the situation
Clarity was never understood
It's a untrustworthy world
Where loyalty can cheat on truth
Distant itself from fairness
No explanation was needed
Just an ejaculation of deceit
Domestic violence became internal silence
Nobody can hear the screams
Truth gave oral sex to lies
Then one day
Just one day
The tables are turn
Happiness was the outcome
When both minds tolerated respect
Kisses of sincerity laid pecks on gratitude neck
Romance made love again
Then passion gave flowers to sincere hugs

QUEST TO FIND YOUR HEART

I never wanted to hold a woman's hand until I seen you
A thought of romance within a moment that consists of passion
My feelings are true
They are like clouds sliding across the sky that's blue
Then your smile brightens of my garden
Making every flower blossom into their purpose
When I see your beauty, I feel so nervous
I'm mesmerized by your eyes as you look at me
I'm trying to comprehend my lost path to your heart
It's like I need a map to get to your love
Can you leave a message in a bottle?
That way if I decide to take a swim in the ocean
I know deep down in my soul there's hope we will be together

COLD ARROW

It was a cold brisk night where Cupid shot his arrow
I was hurt so bad when the dart stung
The confusion set in as the arrow miss my heart and pierce my lung
My heart is broken from a miss opportunity
Then Saddens sets in as the moon brightens up the night
I'm really hurt, and I can't do anything about it
I just got to be patient until my blessings are granted
It's like a garden that needs seeds to be planted

MISSING LOVE

I miss holding your hand taking a long walk
Then I felt the warmth from your palms that I was safe and
secure with you
So when I turned to look into your eyes
My heart was smiling every time it beat so slowly
You made me happy with your energy that I miss you when
I'm with you
I love you with my soul that my spirit grows like flowers
when you water me with sincere love.

HOPELESS ROMANCE

I can stare deep inside your eyes wondering your thoughts
Then you blink slowly where I stop wondering
I saw a shine that made my heart flutter
You are in love with my presence
I'm in love with your presence
We share the same agenda then a moment of clarity pauses us
I want to make love to you and showcase my love
Taking my time to express my emotions with every kiss
You begin to shed tears accepting my arrow
I'm your Cupid as I fly my love across your soul
Our bodies become one with each other
You fell deeper in love with my presence
I fell deeper in love with your presence
As long as we are together our love will forever last

A SAD DREAM

These dreams became false realities to the thoughts that consumes me
I came to the realization my heart is destined to be broken
You are my soulmate that died in my future
I'm not happy no more with love because it became homeless in my heart
It's like you can love someone so much that you forget you are alone
Many times, I can feel the distance from my spirit to yours
Other times I can fall deep in a dark place of unhappiness
I'm saddened by the lack of not knowing what's going to happen
I can't trust no one with my heart anymore
It's an emotion that sails so far in the middle of the sea
That many can't see how much hurt I endured during these times
So now I got to place my feelings inside a sacred closed institution
My security has no guard and now I'm vulnerable to being hurt forever.

CORAL SPIRIT

I'll dive into the deepest part of the ocean

Not even the sharks wanted to take a bite

They felt my sadness through the ocean current

It's like they wanted me to drown in my own sorrow

I'll be lost at sea where no one would ever find me

At least I'll be dead without the worries of the world

My soul will become a coral reef

Then I'll be embedded onto the ocean floor

No one can tarnish my memory but only the fish will love me

POOR NEGRO

I can feel poverty in my soul like tears leaving a homeless man's eyes
Nothing can change my thoughts as my stomach growl at night
The times that I was so thirsty, the rain quench me

The poverty in my soul is like a tragedy touching a family of a lost one
The days brought internal pain from not having proper clothes
I can feel the distant from the planet to where I wanted to go back to god

I know poverty like ancient remedies of medicine to cure the sick
Those ancient remedies couldn't heal a broken soul
A soul that was so shattered that my spiritual puzzle was missing a piece

I not only know poverty well, but it begins inside my heart
when I accepted the conditions
Will poverty ever end inside my mind that's shackle with
hate from the past?

Can I trust the future negro to not follow my thoughts?
Will my history cure the future poverty-stricken world?

Poverty consume me that I need to unshackle my mind
That way my abdomen won't rumble at night but the food for
my thoughts secure the souls of my legacy.

DEATH TO LOVE

This pain hurts so bad that these tears are bleeding

I can't stop crying to the point my heart is buried

Its laying in a plot next to my emotions

Can this be death to my heart?

I'm not ready to die from this hurt

I want to live longer so I can resurrect my ability to love.

A SHACKLED HEART

Tonight, I am sad and alone

My heart is floating in the middle of the sea

I never felt like I would lose hope

I'm shackled where only God can set me free

He holds the keys to this sadden heart

It's like My soul is tired from fighting these hurtful chains

I want to be happy and at peace

Can someone come and release me from this pain?

A PEACEFUL DREAM

As I close my eyes, I once visualize an angel
She reminded me of you from your beautiful smile
Your radiant glow dimmed the sun rays
Not a single cloud flew pass your sunshine
Then I heard your voice so well it's like a whisper from God
You announce a Queen has arrived
I begin to kneel to your royal spirit
I'm a servant to your heart to whereas I'll cater to your soul
I'm happy with your presence, it keeps me calm
You are my Forever sanctuary
Every time I close my eyes, you are my angelic tranquility.

INNER OCEAN

I dived deep inside my inner self to realize I have four beautiful fishes
I discovered love, gratitude, sincerity, and humbleness
They all have many different traits, but they all have the ability to swim my greatness to shore
That's because my spiritual waves are calm.

BEGINNING OF THE END

I trusted you with my soul then you broke a bond
My tears are evaporated into heaven because my heart is shattered

I believe you were different by the way you made me smile
Then my happiness had an alter ego which was sadness

Now I understand why I'm hurt because you were hurt
Our love died when I found out you wasn't healed

My closure will only come when I accept the ending
I deserve true happiness I never should've overlook the beginning

MENTAL STORM

I can foresee comfort from within
These dark days comes like clouds to the sky
It's like waiting for the storm to arrive
I can see the sky turning black now
The temperature is changing drastically
The wind is blowing so rapidly
I can feel the rain drops as they tap the top of my head
The lightening is causing a piece of my anxiety to determine my moment
This storm needs to pass without harm
Now the thunder is pounding hard
Creating a battle with my thoughts
I need shelter from this experience
Then I look up and saw a glimpse of the sun
The thoughts in my mind seems quiet now
My inner cries told the universe I needed some peace
So now I can function for the rest of the day.

JOYFUL

What gives me so much joy?

It's the value I see in others as they see it in themselves

What gives me so much joy?

When others smile brightens up their sad days

What gives me so much joy?

Listening to the words of triumph that one endured

What gives me so much joy?

The blessings many achieve when they did not expect it

What gives me so much joy?

That I can inspire and motivate others to be better.

A CRYING DEED

That young lady seems so disturbed
Her face is saddened by something that's bothering her
What should I do to help her in this time of need?
It's like her thoughts wants to speak
Her eyes begin to rain from the internal pain
She's lost in a character that don't exist
I was cautious to ask her any questions
She was demolished by something I didn't even know
Then she screamed God help me as she covers her face in her hands
Young lady is there something I can do to help?
She didn't respond not knowing my purpose
I told her whatever it is try to find the good out of it
Then she responded I can't because I lost a dear friend
I ask her what was the last thing she said to you?
She replied by saying her friend stated she love her and want the best for her
The Good is in her message now it's up to you to be the best because she loves you
Then her frown begins to smile as she said thank you sir

I never had anyone tell me something so profound
You are welcome I never want to see anyone down
Just promise me you will do the same if you see a hurt person
We all in need of uplifting and healing is contagious.

DIFFERENT SEASONS

I'm alone fighting all my battles as one
The love many have are just words that sounds good
Their actions reveal the opposite
It's like reading the glossary before the book
What did I do to deserve this type of behavior?
I don't need a savior
All I need is support and the love of you all
The same support and love that I'm passionate to give
Then it hit me one quiet night
My season with these people has passed
I'm fall and their summer
My spiritual leaves are falling off the trees
Their leaves are full of life
In many cases I can be the cold blizzard
While others are the showers produce in spring
It's time to move on from such confusion weather
I need to be in the same season to feel completed from others.

BARE FLOOR

I laid many nights on the cold floor wondering my next move

My mental chess pieces weren't available

It was like the board was empty and no one would play

All I could do is cry myself to sleep

Laying in a position like a baby missing their mom

My eyes were closed hoping my dreams was peaceful

Thinking to myself, why is my dreams real and my reality is fake

Then I woke up from this cold floor

I've never had a good night sleep because I lost everything

What is God trying to tell me?

I can't keep laying like this

What did I miss?

I don't know what to do anymore

My tears abandoned me as well as my feelings for others

I lost myself in the midst of being cold with no spiritual blanket

Then one morning I woke up and the heat was on

My empty board produce many pieces

Then I realize the best move I could make was letting it all go.

DEAR EARTH

It's many obstacles that challenges the spirits of today
You can be in a higher plane of thought
Then you can be in a dark place
The nights can be a brisk of cold
Whereas the days can be hot from the truths you told
The earth has evolved more than before
Sometimes the plants don't grow because of the lack of care
Then the bees don't produce honey because life is not sweet
It's like the prophets haven't told this type of story
Many truths weren't discussed with the new world
How can we survive the poverty?
When will the killings stop?
The diseases are so normal now to where we don't have enough medicine
Many times, the seasons are confused by the directions of the globe
What are we going to do?
How can we make food safe and healthy again?
There's only one cure for this earth

That's love because when love is involved then there's no malice.

YOU ARE

You are very special to me

It was your aura when we first met

I was addicted to your energy

The way you walk with confidence of a Queen

I bow my head at your feet

You are a quiet storm to my heart

I find shelter in my thoughts

The moments of holding your hand

Opening up doors so the world knows

You are a rare form of a woman

You have an ancestry persona

It's like my dreams are nightmares if I don't see your face

I want you one day in my space

A slow kiss to secure your heart

Those eyes tell many stories

I want to be a chapter in your book of love.

A DREAM OF CLOSURE

As I awaken this morning, I cried in my sleep
It was strange I had no tears, I didn't even count no sheep
All I counted was the hurt and pain that you left inside of me
Then God spoke to me with his firm strong voice
It was a trumpet with a soothing reasoning to my heart
He reveals many chapters in my life with you
I was saddened by the spiritual movie I was watching
Then I realize that I was hurting myself more by staying
These feelings I have and had were and are real
Then his voice spoke louder as he told me not to think or feel
Just lay peacefully in your sleep as I continue to reveal
Beauty is in the eyes of the beholder but most importantly in the hearts of that same beholder
Your heart was blinded that you couldn't see the pain inside of her
As you were healing, she wasn't feeling the same love
Your sincerity was too much as your gratefulness showed her selfishness
My son I molded someone that's for your soul, but you need to let go

In conclusion you need to keep your composure
As I ease your mind and the hurt of this pain it's time you get your closure.

MENTALLY TOGETHER

I've been distant because when I'm near you I'm alone
I only feel together with you when I'm sitting thinking about our happiness.

GEMINI CHRONICLES

I'm lost in my own mind that my thoughts talk to me
My inner friend speaks to me with a caution voice
Then my outer friend interrupts him as his voice speeds to communicate
I'm confused by my thoughts they create anxiety
I need to choose one friend because their voices are too loud
They are battling each other to control my thoughts
My anxiety takes a swing at pts. and now I have a migraine
I'm mentally tired that my good traits and bad traits are conflicting
Who can I be? Which me am I going to be?
I'm getting depress from the gloomy ambience
The world is uncertain by characteristics that my Jekyll always Hyde
Then Hyde didn't hide he just can't adapt to this sensitive world
Now I'm having a panic attack because I fear my next thoughts
I wish my brain could take a break so my horoscope could rest

I need some peace from my consistent persona of restless

That my aura can be socially in a place of serenity.

FALL SEASON

It's a strange day seeing the leaves changing colors
You can hear them talk as you walk on them
A moment to embrace the conversation you had with the earth
While I pause to enjoy the beauty of colors that attracts me
I start to think about how a tree could die but produce life
The squirrels rumbling through the covered ground looking for nuts
Then the birds chirp on a naked branch
It was so many colors that it looks like I was opening a crayon box
The browns, yellows, orange, and green
I remain pause wiping my face trying to figure out why
Then I begin to smile because I figured it out that the earth is clean.

LETTER TO CUPID

Dear Cupid, can you please come and get your arrow?
It was snatch out of my heart
Then it was thrown on the ground as I grab my chest
The blood is pouring out my heart as I look at the arrow as it covers with my love
I'm on my knees pleading with the universe why is this happening
I have so many emotions leaking from an area of happiness
So, Cupid please come and get this arrow so I can heal from many moments of hurt
It is like I'm dying from the disappointment and deceit
I need a soulful bandage to cover my pain
So, in closing, I deserve happiness with the respect of love
When you come, I'll be on the ground next to a piece of my heart
Gasping for God to heal my distress and discomfort
Thank you from the dying happiness

A LOVABLE PURPOSE

I'm so in love that when I look up at the sky the clouds form shapes of hearts
Then an airplane crosses them like an arrow shot by Cupid
When I look up again the sky was clear
It was so empty that the wind blew invisible clouds
All I can vision is her smile shining creating a rainbow
She's so full of life that her energy keeps the sun bright
I'm so in love with her that my heart begins to warm with her touch
It's like a butterfly landing on my arm
I am at peace when speaks words of encouragement
This that type of love that will only last when I kiss you in front of God

SAVORING LOVE
(FT. POET ALIADA DUNCAN)

Devoured by devotion

You are my potion

I drink until drunkenness has drenched me

I thirst, but you have quenched me

My man, my magic

My hobby, my habit

Your warmth so poetic and potent

My key, I am open

This poem tastes like love

Gumbo, sweet potato pie & cornbread

I am full, I am fed

Food for my soul

This poem is rich

Rubies, royalty and gold

And you, my man my love

We transcend dimensions together

It fits so well, like a glove

The juice—and you drip all over me

A serine scene—serenity
I have bathed in his divine divinity

Devoured by her devotion
I feed her my potion
This entrée of love
I can taste the same feast
The love she instills in me
I am full—
Digested trust and loyalty
Then I look across the table
I see longevity—
A piece of calm
You've completed my mission
I'm in a place of tranquility
It is like a glimpse at the moon
Hopefully forever will be soon
My soul reacts to your spirit
A moment where effort makes love to perfection
I'm safe in your heart as it beats to correction

Correcting past regressions

My woman, my lesson

FALLING PROMISE

I laid many nights alone visualizing forever comfort with you
Then I turn my head on the pillow feeling vacant from your heart
So, I question my ability to lead your soul to my spirit
You create many happy pictures in my head
It seems like an eternity of love when you speak of my greatness
Then I turn my head again on the same pillow you promise a lifetime
I'm confuse by the words that don't add up to the visuals
This a moment where I not only question again but answered
Could this be that I am just a comfort for you?
Why put me through love when you don't want in love
It's like I'm lost in my own heart
Maybe I'm just a bird that flies alone
I never will land because there is no branch in the world of hurt
The skies are the only thing that makes me happy
It's time to fall in love with my own flight so when I do decide to land

My soulmate will be waiting to secure my wings

WINSTON SALEM

A peaceful thought knowing she stays really far
I will travel many times to embrace her heart
She gives me a glimpse of what tranquility could be
Her eyes capture my inner peace
I can see myself holding her near
That type of security that erases her fears
She deserves to be catered to
I want to pamper her soul
Give her more than the world
The universe is the destination where I want Cupid to shoot me
Then take the arrow and plant it in the ground of forever
I'm in love with the thoughts of being with a warm spirit
Winston Salem has a calming wind that blew her to me
My heart is the trees that grew from the roots of her love

MR POET

As I sit at a club in Harlem during the Harlem Renaissance
I'm relaxing hearing his voice
Each word is articulated with the sounds of a historic leader
I can understand the literacy of jazz poetry
As he speaks louder the cadence sounds like a trumpet
The waitress brought my cocktail to my table
Her smile was so radiant from the lights shining on the stage
Then I shed so many tears hearing The Negro Speaks of Rivers
I can feel my soul shiver
The power in the words as he delivers
Then he stops as the audience faces are in a shock
The moment multiple people began to stand and applaud
Then he waves us to settle down he have much more to say
As he thanks us all for coming to support, he offers autographs before we leave
I'm so nervous and happy at the same time
I can talk to my idol, inspiration and the reason why I would write in the future
Then I got closer to the table my hands are shaking

I can't wait to tell him how much I love his work
That I'm going to be a poet one day
He reaches out his hand and said how are you
Then before I could shake his hand and speak
I woke up in cold sweats knowing my dream came true

SAND

Every step I take I wrote I love you as the water removes my footprints
The beach is my canvas to show the world my feelings for you
So I decided to make a sculpture of a heart
I can vision my love for you to be forever
Knowing I use gods earth to express my love for you.

LIVING DREAM

As I sit on this park bench thinking
I can see the squirrels run from the grass to the trees
Living their purpose as they collect their nuts
Then I realized Falling in love with a dream can hurt your reality
You tend to reach for help when the other arm is still by their side
I don't have the opportunity, but I have the ability to happy
Then the squirrel in me can run from my past to my future
Maybe I'm collecting the wrong nuts

RELAXING BATH

My mind is clog from all these thoughts
Worrying about the stresses of the world
Then it hit me I need to relax my mind
Let me turn on the warm water
Before I put the plug in, I need to light me some candles
Grab my phone so I can have me some slow jazz
Adding the bubbles in the bath now I'm almost complete
The mood is almost set to where I'm on a mental vacation
Pouring some wine is the last step before I step into relaxation
Now I sit here with my eyes closed allowing this positivity to take my body over
My mind, body and soul feels like a night on the beach
I'm in the cosmos as my aura is full of euphoria
I cannot remember why I was so mentally tired
I'm secured as long as my mind is tranquilized

WOMAN

She is so sophisticated that when I see her, I'm stuck
It's like time stop and the only vision was her beauty
Then time return and each click I think about her ambition
Her ability to inspire one's self with her aura
She has strength but it comes from with in
The confidence of her personality
I'm humble in her presence
Something like a servant to her every needs
A powerful woman
That every man walks by with the thoughts of wanting her
But I'm so into her that I need her
Take her hand and walk her to the place where she sits
A throne of sincerity

THAT FEELING

I know that feeling
You know that wanting Love
That I deserve that love
Just a simple hug
Where you secure my spirit with your soul
To as when I sleep you watch my breath
As my heart beats because I'm dreaming of you love
The rubbing your feet because you walk through my mind love
Just daydreaming of making love to you
To where each stroke has its own emotion love
So, I definitely understand your love
That divine moment to where you look into my eyes and you trust me
To love you because I love me

LOST BATTLE

Why didn't you fight for me?
Why didn't you fight for us?
Place your trust into Gods plan knowing you would be loved
Understanding that trials may come but the tribulations was minor
I'm the man you always wanted
The man you dreamed about when your beautiful eyes closed at night
When you awakened in the morning, I was the man you needed
Why stay?
Did contentment keep you from longevity of happiness?
Why bury me in a tomb of pain to where I can't resurrect into peace
I'm so hurt
My cries scream for help to where my tears have tears
Was I not good enough?
Were you afraid to change your life to have a better life?
I prayed to God every night for you to be my security

I feel like I'm lost in a forest and the grass keeps going as I walk to find you

Did you ever feel any feelings for me?

You said you trust me?

I would've led you to water and took a sip, so you know there is no danger

Now all I have is my feelings battling my thoughts

Where do I go from here knowing you loved another?

I should have stayed away if I knew you would have left before you even came.

PROTECTION

As she laid across the bed, I realize she is not comfortable
I decided to relax her mind
I wanted to make sure she was at peace
Then I proceeded to tell her how much I appreciated her
That my heart was lost without her laying on my chest
She gives me rhythm with every beat
I am alive When I'm in her presence
Her smile is so radiant that she lights up the dark room
I whispered soft words into her ears that massage her spirit
The energy begins to soothe her so gently
She uttered thank you with a voice of serenity
Then I kiss her forehead because it's the smartest part of her brain
I wanted to secure her thoughts
As she closed her eyes so effortlessly
I pray that she dreams I am her guardian angel
So, when she awakens in the morning then she will know her soul is forever protected.

DEAR LOVE

When you left me, I was shattered by the confusion
I never felt so much pain that it seems like I'm dying
Why did you leave me like this?
My heart is distant from my feelings
It's like I am on the moon and my soul is crying on earth
The ocean are my tears expressing my agony
I cannot understand why you took the arrow back and place it in your bag
Did you not believe in my ability to love?
Your lack of confidence took away my confidence
I'm scrapping every moment to move forward
Then my thoughts took many steps backwards
I'm crying so much that the ocean is flooding my thoughts
It's like my spirit is in a state of an emergency
I have no answers anymore to these questions
I feel like just giving up on you because you failed me
Do you have anything to say?
Would you try and shoot me with your arrow again?
I just want to love someone unconditionally

I would feel failed knowing a future with a woman is part of my purpose
Sincerely a man who is ready for forever.

FAR TOUCH

It was a cold brisk windy day and all I could do was think about you
All I needed was your touch to secure my soul
I never felt this confused on why I am lost without you near me
I can't focus on my reasoning because My wanders
Your eyes create a mesmerizing attraction
I'm hypnotized every time I look inside them
They hold many secrets to the questions in my head
Your lips are so soft the clouds become jealous
So, I yearned for them to give me magical moments
I crave for your body to allow me to make love to your soul
Every stroke has purpose and energy to conquer your heart
I just need your touch to make a sculpture of forever
It just seems so unreal because you are far away
In my dream is where you stay but in my life you live forever.

CRY TO SLEEP

I'm so lost that my tears disappeared in the sky

I've drowned in my own thoughts

No one can save my soul because I'm alone

Stranded on an island without the tools to survived

All my clues sailed across the ocean in a bottle

I don't want to die alone not knowing if someone even tried to save me

I'll forever not Rest in Peace

So, I continue to cry even though my tears evaporated inside my heart

I am Mentally tired from the pain that consumes me

I'll just stop running and take a seat by this tree

Hopefully, I'll cry myself to sleep

That way when I wake, I'll know someone tried to rescue me.

THOUGHTFUL EYES

I visualized this woman who have a beautiful radiant smile
The type of smile that makes the sun so jealous
She brightens up my day even when she doesn't even know
Then I realized This same woman I have not seen in a while
is hidden in a different world
How can I travel to her heart? Land my spirit on her soul
She is so beautiful that my eyes miss her so dearly
Then I realized she has a love
All I have Is thoughts of her being my love
So, I decided to take a nap knowing she will appear
Taking trips to places only people could imagine
As I awaken from this peaceful nap, I didn't see her anymore
It is easy to fall in love with a dream only to be alone in the
nightmare of reality.

APOLOGETIC HEART

I'm so sorry for loving so hard that I push the love of your life away

I was worried that I was going to be hurt and a heartbreak is not needed

Do you forgive me?

I know your loneliness is because of my inability to love again

My feelings are valid, and I want to be happy as well

There were times where you spoke to me when you depended on me

Can you please forgive me?

I promise when Cupid shoots another arrow, I'll be ready for another chance

You deserve to be loved and I deserve to be warm

This will be the last time I jeopardize your happiness for my lack of understanding

Sincerely your heart that you can trust again.

FOREVER DREAM

It's nights where I just want to sleep
You are My supreme dream
You are similar to perfection
My eyes recognize a graceful woman
Then I woke up quietly
I couldn't even talk nor could I see you
The nightmare begins
I really Miss my forever friend
It's days like this where I hurry to bed
So, I can get the chance to take you on a date
A nice walk on the lake holding hands
Then Your kisses melt my heart
At this particular moment it dawned on me
I never been this happy
The universe connected two souls
It's like the sun made love to the moon
This point in time was perfected
The thought of having a picnic on Venus was so refreshing
I fed you my spirit And You fed me your soul
Then reality sets in when the alarm clocks rings

I came to the conclusion
You were my forever dream.

FINAL KISS

I've closed my eyes tonight wondering will tomorrow bring your heart to me
Then my first dream told many stories
I lost you internally in my sea of love to where I have no boat to come and get you
All I have is the short memories that created longevity thoughts of forever
Your soft kisses reminded me of happiness to come
That is why I always wanted them because they brought me peace
My feelings are trapped in a place of untrustworthy
You did not fight for the love I had for you and the peace you deserved
Now I'm lost in the ocean wondering why you didn't sail to my pain
My dream turned nightmare when I realized I only drowned because you really did not like me like how you portrayed
I may not die in your arms tonight, but I was Alive in my own soul
So be careful and mindful the next time you kiss another

Every peck has emotions and memories
The thought of love can be sincere if you look that person in the eyes after you kiss.

CRASHING UNIVERSE

As I sit inside my own head, I can hear sounds from the
thoughts of pain
The screams come from the deep part of my soul
It rose to the top of my heart
The beats pounds drastically
You can see the drama in the hurt
Each pound produces crying blood
I am having a heart attack
She left me without a pulse
I'm dying in a thought of tortured
My eyes rolls in the back of head
The pain increases making my spirit suffer from the
unhappiness that is endured
My head is hurting
My eyes are crying
My heart is bleeding
I'm in a state of melancholy
I never Hurt this bad
Sadness consumes my aura
Will it end?

Will trauma create forever damage?
My hands cover my face
I'm ashamed, hurt, embarrassed, confused
This cannot be the outcome of a lost love
It seems like the ocean left the shoreline
The sun hides behind the clouds until the sky turns black
Then the moon placed it's shine behind the same clouds
Many stars have no purpose
I can feel my universe die from a crater of separation.

DYING VOICE

I am so fed up

Frustrated by the beatings that I can feel from my ancestor's past

My ribs have generational trauma

My great grandfather was brutally assaulted by a Klansman

They wanted to hang him

So every time I get a migraine that is his spirit begging them to stop

Nobody had camera phones, all they had was futuristic visions

These visions created nightmares that produced PTSD

My eyes are damaged from the cops

Letting a dog bite the legs of innocent people

Then we had to choose between where we can drink water

Don't go chasing waterfalls became the norm based on how fire hydrants are now weapons

They are drowning us with hate and evil

Now They use tasers as the electrical punishment

Increasing voltages depending on how black your skin color

But when we use our voice, they take it away

They barely can hear us because of the lack of oxygen in our spirits

I can't breathe, but my heart beats then my lungs collapsed for what they did to me

I'm black and I'm proud

I'm Proud to be Black because that is who I am

I gave this country so much of me

Enlistment in the U.S Army, are you proud Uncle Sam?

A hurt black man with feelings

A stress black man with emotions

A strong back man with goals

A dedicated black man with life

What have we done to you all to get this treatment?

I have a voice, but it gets silent and silent to where I'm quiet

I am dying because every time we try to utilize our voices

You all suffocate us with your hate and injustices

So I lay in pool of being black in America

Nobody wants to save us from this everlasting misery

The concrete is a walking cemetery of black souls that was black people

Now I took my final breath from dying without voice

I just hope the next generation can get the CPR this culture needs so we can breathe.

UNEXPECTED FEELINGS

Many nights I've wanted you here close inside my arms

I can secure your emotions with consistent warmth

How can I miss someone who I never glance my eyes on?

I'm confused by the moments of believing

This woman is so special

Like a gift handed to me from Gods present

Then my past consumes her thoughts

If I could change I will

Then my thoughts consume me

Does she think about me?

I just want a night of romance to create a spark in her heart

She never thought I wanted to make love to her mind

Who is this woman that lives in my world?

The same woman I wanted to cherish

Show her things her eyes never seen

I want to be her tour guide into forever happiness.

SLEEPLESS SEX

These Nights of anxiety

Insomnia consumes my night

The visions of another man inside you

My future dreams are dead

The present nightmares I'm having are overwhelming

I can hear your moans as he penetrates you

This can't be true, it just can't

I'm a nervous wreck

My heart is bleeding from being vandalized by lust

The moans are getting louder and louder

Your body goes into a shock

His ejaculation and your orgasm I cannot trust

I can't even cry myself to sleep

My breath is blown away

I'm having a panic attack

Each beat of my heart has an irregular rhythm

I'm dying in my own thoughts

It's like My soul has been shattered

Closing my eyes peacefully is a goal

It hurts knowing you made lust when I wanted to make love.

GODS HANDS

God place his hands into the earth and molded you

A special seed that connect to the soul that form a root

Your skin is brown like the water touching the shore

Your hair begins to sprout like a tree releasing its branches

God begin to shape your eyes like his vision of an angel

They are very keen like an eagle soaring above the sky

Then he rubs his hands so slow to create your nose

You can sense positive energy with your aura

You are so beautiful

The world is awaiting this queen

Finally a storm was forming to where God reach to the sky

Took two clouds and shape your lips

They are full of magic from the thunder

Now the earth is flooding but your lips remain soft

Your words flow with articulation from the blessings of the sounds of trumpets

God yell to heavens then he whispers to the earth

All hail comes a Queen who will place in others' lives as their peace

Then you smiled and promise God you will fulfill your purpose

Today a beautiful creation was perfected when God place his hands into the earth.

GUITAR STRINGS OF LIFE

He pulls out his guitar pick and gave the crowd an arrogant smirk

He picks the strings to tease the listeners

Now he leans back on the stool to turn the amplifier up

Took a sip of some vodka then he winks at the lady in the front row

I knew his passion was about to be showcased

He played a tune that sounded sad full of a melancholy mood

I became slump over as each rhythm trigger the pain inside

I remained calmed and nodded my head

He knows his fingers are creating thoughts

We all are in different feelings

I know my emotions are beating on a cadence of pain

The lady next to me whisper what's wrong

I explained he's playing my life.

A HUMBLE DEATH

I prayed many moons I wouldn't be in this situation

My face made love to the concrete causing a painful relationship

Why do this keep happening to only us?

What did we do so wrong that we are being murdered?

Now I am laying wondering how quick my death will be

I've lived my life so far doing all the great things

To be here with my eyes blurry seeing my own people filming me

I can't breathe as my life starts to realize it's demised

I also prayed many moons ago that if I'm in this situation

My people would feel my energy of positivity

They will help me and not let this death occur

I can hear screams and yelling

Will this possible murder be halted?

I don't want to die like this in the middle of street

Please someone who hears this weaken voice crying and begging for help

My eyes are closing so fast that I can't see the phones anymore

I never prayed for this outcome

The moon didn't reveal the dark clouds I was facing

I died tonight alone, afraid and saddened

The world becomes outrage and chaotic

My corpse made history and became famous

In due time I'll be just a name because someone who looks like me will be famous as well.

CHAOTIC DREAMS

I had many dreams

Counting hearts as they jump souls

You came into my life with peace

The kind of peace that I needed to settle these chaotic nights

The feeling of being safe is what I felt the minute I laid my eyes on you

I was secure as your eyes warm my heart

Then I was confined to a place of serenity

We begin to meditate to silence to where the chaos died

I came to ease the pain that I saw hidden beneath the surface

A soul so pure that can still love again

I just need to pray to God to amend my heart

Take the pain away because I want to love again

And while my mind says one thing pulling me left

My heart knows that this isn't a mistake

Listening for God's confirmation

Allowing each internal scripture to connect to me

I yearn for your love to be manifested

Leave the past is the past and let me help remove any insecurities

Love me while I love you unconditionally

The foundation of our future depends on the present truths.

Lightning Source UK Ltd.
Milton Keynes UK
UKHW020941061020
371099UK00012B/437